1 MONTH OF
FREE
READING

at
www.ForgottenBooks.com

By purchasing this book you are eligible for one month membership to ForgottenBooks.com, giving you unlimited access to our entire collection of over 1,000,000 titles via our web site and mobile apps.

To claim your free month visit:

www.forgottenbooks.com/free1301361

ISBN 978-0-428-70989-1
PIBN 11301361

THE

AUDITORS' REPORT

OF THE

RECEIPTS AND EXPENDITURES

OF THE

TOWN OF ANDOVER.

1871-72.

ANDOVER:
PRINTED BY WARREN F. DRAPER.
1872.

THE

AUDITORS' REPORT

OF THE

RECEIPTS AND EXPENDITURES

OF THE

TOWN OF ANDOVER.

1871-72.

ANDOVER:

PRINTED BY WARREN F. DRAPER.

1872.

.

REPORT.

SELECTMEN'S ACCOUNT.

SCHOOLHOUSES.

PAID PER ORDER OF THE SCHOOL COMMITTEE :

HIGH SCHOOL.

Holt and Higgins, pail,	$ 40	
William Barnett, repairs,	1 30	
		$1 70

GRAMMAR SCHOOL.

Robert Callahan, padlock,	$ 50	
Holt and Higgins, brushes,	1 60	
J. L. Hammett, furniture,	30 00	
E. H. Barnard, repairs,	5 67	
Bridget Abercrombie, cleaning,	9 54	
Horace Wilson, repairs,	5 64	
William Barnett, supplies,	4 00	
Abbott and Jenkins, repairs,	19 48	
Stephen Kenney, repairs on pump,	7 40	
L. A. Cooper, repairs on blackboards,	6 25	
		90 08
Amount carried forward,		$91 78

FRYE DISTRICT.

Amount brought forward,		$91 78
E. Francis Holt, repairs,	$4 07	
Henry Boynton, cleaning,	3 40	
Jonathan Poor, repairs,	14 25	
W. O. Haskell and Co., chairs,	6 00	
E. H. Barnard, repairs,	2 22	
Thomas Clark, repairs,	1 00	
		30 94

HOLT DISTRICT.

Henry C. Harnden, repairs,	14 25	
J. E. Whiting, repairs on clock,	1 00	
		15 25

SOUTH CENTRE DISTRICT.

H. W. French, rent of land,	2 00	
Holt and Higgins, supplies,	4 09	
J. L. Hammett, books,	3 60	
Stephen Kenney, repairs on pump,	1 50	
Robert Callahan, repairs,	1 00	
W. O. Haskell and Co., settees,	3 90	
E. H. Barnard, repairs,	4 48	
Bridget Abercrombie, cleaning,	6 00	
Horace Wilson, repairs,	17 33	
William Barnett, stove, etc.,	55 23	
		99 13

VILLAGE DISTRICT.

J. A. Smart, insurance,	40 00	
L. A. Cooper, repairs on blackboard,	10 00	
E. H. Barnard, repairs,	3 42	
J. E. Whiting, repairs on clock,	1 00	
Bridget Abercrombie, cleaning,	6 00	
Horace Wilson, repairs,	6 75	
William Barnett, stoves and supplies,	51 05	
		118 22
Amount carried forward,		$355 32

OSGOOD DISTRICT.

Amount brought forward,		$355 32
Joseph Abbott, chair,	$1 50	
Henry Boynton, repairs,	70	
J. A. Smart, insurance,	30 00	
		32 20

PHILLIPS DISTRICT.

E. H. Barnard, repairs,	60	
H. S. Greene, repairs,	5 60	
		6 20

BALLARD VALE DISTRICT.

H. S. Greene, repairs,	48 69	48 69

SCOTLAND DISTRICT.

H. S. Greene, repairs,	120 33	
John B. Abbott, repairs,	5 40	
		125 73

WEST CENTRE DISTRICT.

E. Francis Holt, labor,	2 00	
Samuel Woodman, chairs,	2 25	
A. C. Richardson, fence,	3 11	
Henry Boynton, cleaning,	2 92	
E. H. Barnard, repairs,	81 47	
Abbott and Jenkins,	253 88	
William Barnett, stove, etc.,	21 70	
		367 33

NORTH DISTRICT.

Henry Boynton, cleaning,	1 25	
Joseph Abbott, chair,	1 25	
		2 50
Amount carried forward,		$937 97

BAILEY DISTRICT.

Amount brought forward,		$937 97
Henry Boynton, supplies,	1 96	
Fannie A. Hardy, cleaning,	2 00	
E. C. Upton, repairs,	5 00	
Miles Flint, repairs,	3 00	
		11 96

ABBOTT DISTRICT.

Hattie R. Abbott, sundries,	2 80	
Joseph Abbott, chair,	1 75	
Almon P. Abbott, painting,	56 00	
Henry Boynton, repairs,	1 36	
John R. Loring, repairs on pump,	1 50	
		63 41
Total Amount,		$1013 34

SCHOOLS.

PAID PER ORDER OF THE SCHOOL COMMITTEE :

HIGH SCHOOL.

S. C. Smith, teaching,	$1000 00	
Sara E. Merrill, teaching,	346 00	
Ellis and Snow, use of piano,	15 00	
F. A. Dawson, diplomas,	25 00	
Thomas Smith, janitor,	50 00	
W. F. Draper, books,	13 62	
		$1449 62

GRAMMAR SCHOOL.

D. D. Smith, teaching,	666 00	
Rosa L. Pratt, teaching,	459 99	
Hannah W. Smith, teaching,	200 00	
Agnes H. Donald, teaching,	120 00	
Amount carried forward,	$1445 99	$1449 62

Amount brought forward,	$1445 99	$1449 62
Katie W. Cooke, teaching,	$100 00	
Ellen T. Brown, teaching,	82 22	
Abby Carter, teaching music,	24 00	
Robert Callahan, janitor,	72 00	
Ellis and Snow, use of piano,	30 00	
J. M. Richards, use of piano,	27 00	
John Cornell, coal,	102 75	
John Chandler, wood,	19 76	
W. F. Draper, books,	17 80	
Ezra Farnham, sawing wood,	3 91	
Holt and Higgins, supplies,	3 58	
William Callahan, sawing wood,	5 00	
Oliver Ditson, books,	1 00	
		1935 01

ABBOTT DISTRICT.

Hattie R. Abbott, teaching,	266 66	
Joshua H. Chandler, wood,	29 47	
John M. Bailey, wood,	10 50	
A. N. Luscomb, wood,	4 75	
Isaac Carruth, wood,	4 60	
E. Francis Holt, sawing wood,	6 00	
Henry Boynton, supplies,	2 40	
W. F. Draper,	49	
		324 87

SCOTLAND DISTRICT.

Agnes H. Donald, teaching,	199 99	
Fannie E. Callahan, teaching,	108 00	
John B. Abbott, wood,	36 35	
E. P. Hackett, fires,	5 00	
H. S. Greene, supplies,	3 25	
W. F. Draper, books,	50	
		353 09
Amount carried forward,		$4062 59

OSGOOD DISTRICT.

Amount brought forward,		$4062 59
M. A. Whitehouse, teaching,	$366 66	
Jedediah Burtt, wood,	17 00	
Isaac Carruth, wood,	12 68	
Henry Boynton, sawing wood, and supplies,	7 20	
E. Francis Holt, janitor,	4 00	
W. F. Draper, books,	1 45	
Holt and Higgins, supplies,	94	
		409 93

PHILLIPS DISTRICT.

Margie B. Tenney, teaching,	200 00	
Margie B. Tenney, janitor,	8 00	
Lizzie B. Abbott, teaching,	160 00	
Hattie B. Hervey, teaching,	120 00	
Hattie B. Hervey, janitor,	3 00	
Sylvester Abbott, wood,	46 63	
W. F. Draper, books,	1 75	
H. S. Greene, supplies,	1 42	
		540 80

FRYE DISTRICT.

Carrie B. Holt, teaching,	320 50	
Mary E. Jones, teaching,	320 00	
John Cornell, coal,	39 00	
Isaac Carruth, wood,	25 24	
E. Francis Holt, sawing wood,	14 40	
W. F. Draper, books,	9 85	
George L. Stott, janitor,	5 00	
Jonathan Poor, supplies,	1 25	
Holt and Higgins, supplies,	3 92	
		739 16
Amount carried forward,		$5752 48

HOLT DISTRICT.

Amount brought forward,		$5752 48
Anna M. Stoodley, teaching,	$218 00	
Louisa C. Wardwell, teaching,	100 00	
Henry C. Harnden, janitor, and wood,	53 80	
H. S. Greene, supplies,	60	
		372 40

SOUTH CENTRE DISTRICT.

Frances E. Chandler, teaching,	340 00	
Katie A. Findley, teaching,	116 91	
Charlotte H. Abbott, teaching,	100 00	
Irene S. Wardwell, teaching,	120 00	
Fannie E. Callahan, teaching,	55 00	
Clara E. Clement, teaching,	60 00	
John Cornell, coal,	48 75	
Robert Callahan, janitor,	36 00	
John Chandler, wood,	10 09	
Holt and Higgins, supplies,	1 93	
W. F. Draper, books,	4 03	
Ezra Farnham, sawing wood,	3 75	
		896 46

BALLARD VALE DISTRICT.

H. Maria Richardson, teaching,	240 00	
Abbie A. Richardson, teaching,	200 00	
Susie V. Thurston, teaching,	200 00	
Mary E. Bixby, teaching,	120 00	
Hattie E. Abbott, teaching,	120 00	
Mary F. Browne, teaching,	120 00	
J. P. Bradlee, coal,	48 70	
H. S. Greene, janitor and supplies,	54 58	
W. F. Draper, books,	2 02	
P. P. Pillsbury, wood,	7 50	
		1112 80
Amount carried forward,		$8134 14

VILLAGE DISTRICT.

Amount brought forward,		$8134 14
Mary F. Merrill, teaching,	$380 00	
Mary E. Gile, teaching,	320 00	
Katie W. Cooke, teaching,	105 00	
Ella F. Merrill, teaching,	60 00	
John Cornell, coal,	39 00	
John Chandler, wood,	16 30	
George F. Baker, wood,	7 93	
Holt and Higgins, supplies,	8 11	
W. F. Draper, books,	5 65	
Andrew Thompson, janitor,	10 00	
John Sullivan, janitor,	6 00	
Ezra Farnham, sawing wood,	10 77	
		968 76

BAILEY DISTRICT.

Fannie A. Hardy, teaching,	353 33	
William Hardy, wood,	19 00	
John B. Bailey, wood,	10 50	
George Boutwell, wood,	7 13	
Isaac Carruth, wood,	8 53	
W. F. Draper, books,	3 45	
Henry Boynton, supplies,	2 50	
Holt and Higgins, supplies,	68	
		405 12

WEST CENTRE DISTRICT.

Hannah B. Abbott, teaching,	353 32	
Henry Boynton, seats,	127 00	
Joseph Chandler, wood,	25 99	
Daniel L. Trow, wood,	7 60	
E. Francis Holt, wood,	7 75	
E. Francis Holt, janitor and sawing wood,	8 15	
Amount carried forward,	$529 81	$9508 02

Amount brought forward,	$529 81	$9508 02
Frank B. Holt, janitor,	4 00	
W. F. Draper, books,	1 45	
Holt and Higgins, supplies,	69	
		535 95

NORTH DISTRICT.

Hattie P. Hervey, teaching,	166 66	
Annie L. Locke, teaching,	100 00	
A. N. Luscomb, wood,	14 25	
Isaac Carruth, wood,	8 20	
Rufus Bailey, wood,	8 38	
E. Francis Holt, janitor,	4 50	
Henry Boynton, supplies,	3 40	
Holt and Higgins, supplies,	50	
W. F. Draper, books,	3 25	
		309 14
Total Amount,		$10,353 11

SERVICES OF TOWN OFFICERS.

George Foster, School Committee,	$125 00	
E. Francis Holt, School Committee,	150 00	
H. S. Greene, School Committee,	100 00	
Henry Boynton, School Committee,	100 00	
		$475 00
John H. Flint, Selectman, Assessor, and Overseer of the Poor,	275 00	
Benjamin Boynton, Selectman, Assessor, and Overseer of the Poor,	250 00	
Lewis G. Holt, Selectman, Assessor, and Overseer of the Poor,	250 00	
		775 00
John Cornell, engineer,	20 00	
William Bretherick, engineer,	20 00	
James H. Smith, engineer,	20 00	
Joseph W. Poor, engineer,	20 00	
George H. Taylor, engineer,	20 00	
		100 00
John Clark, police,	15 50	
Joshua H. Chandler, police,	12 50	
William Finn, police,	8 00	
Henry Dane, police,	5 00	
Thomas Smith, police,	1 50	
		42 50
E. K. Jenkins, Treasurer,	100 00	
E. K. Jenkins, collecting taxes,	450 00	
		550 00
		$1942 50

STATE AID.

Paid by E. K. Jenkins, Treasurer, $2303 00

TOWN HOUSE.

Thomas Smith, janitor,	$147 00	
Thomas Smith, labor,	4 42	
Abbott and Jenkins, repairs,	82 62	
H. J. Newman, repairs,	18 05	
E. H. Barnard, repairs,	27 98	
William Barnett, repairs,	1 45	
H. P. Beard and Co., supplies,	11 24	
Holt and Higgins, supplies,	1 36	
Smith, Manning, and Co., supplies,	28 43	
John Chandler, wood,	5 90	
George F. Baker, wood,	5 95	
John Cornell, coal,	48 75	
		$383 15

FIRE DEPARTMENT.

ANDOVER STEAMER No. 1.

Pay of members 18 months,	389 50
Poll taxes,	32 00
Oliver W. Hunt, engineer,	93 50
Charles P. Rea, engineer,	78 50
Charles O. Cummings, engineer,	15 00
S. H. Harnden, labor,	4 50
John W. Cochrane, labor,	52 50
John Cornell, coal, supplies, and horses,	180 78
Henry Burtt, horses,	7 00
Albert Marshall, lamps, etc.,	35 50
George E. Smith, curtains,	7 00
H. P. Beard and Co., supplies,	1 13
Smith, Manning, and Co., supplies,	4 59
Holt and Higgins, supplies,	2 10
Amount carried forward,	$903 60

Amount brought forward,	$903 60	
William Barnett, supplies, ·	10 35	
George H. Parker, supplies,	65	
John W. Faulkner, repairs,	16 25	
Charles Mayer, straps and belts,	6 90	
		$937 75

SHAWSHIN No. 2.

Pay of members, 18 months,	860 00	
Poll taxes,	66 00	
Albert E. Clemens, labor,	29 00	
John S. Stark, oil, etc.,	6 33	
F. G. Haynes, supplies,	10 90	
William Bretherick, supplies,	12 50	
Greene and Woodlin, wood,	7 02	
James Smith, sawing wood,	3 50	
Ambrose Howell, labor,	1 50	
Abbott and Jenkins, house as per contract,	1635 92	
William Barnett, stove, etc.,	33 18	
Tucker Manufacturing Co., fixtures,	14 50	
W. O. Haskell and Co., settees and chairs,	48 00	
E. P. Dodge and Co., supplies,	1 00	
J. H. Smith, railroad fare,	1 30	
E. P. Higgins, painting,	75	
J. W. Faulkner, iron work,	75	
Henry W. Abbott, supplies,	2 55	
Samuel Woodman, furniture,	14 99	
		$2749 69

PHILLIPS.

William Raynor, horses,	3 00	
Albert Abbott, supplies,	3 70	
		6 70
Total Amount,		$3694 14

HIGHWAYS.

District.		Expended.	Snow.
1.	John Cornell,	$226 70	$1 00
	Abbott and Jenkins,	6 95	
2.	John R. Loring,	156 00	
	John Driscoll,	29 00	
3.	C. W. Hayward,	169 04	
	J. J. Pearson,	2 34	
4.	N. B. Abbott,	96 80	
5.	W. Hackett,	1 40	
	John B. Abbott,	38 65	
6.	Jaques Gowing,	75 00	
7.	George F. Mason,	73 50	
	J. O. Cheever,	40	4 60
8.	William Jenkins,	30 00	
9.	William Tucker,	117 00	
10.	N. F. Abbott,	175 25	
11.	Wyman D. Hussey,	178 35	
12.	H. P. Holt,	178 00	
	Moody B. Abbott,	11 00	
13.	J. H. Chandler, -	175 00	4 00
14.	E. F. Holt,	141 43	
15.	Joseph T. Lovejoy,	69 85	
16.	Asa W. Livingston,	105 00	
17.	Simeon Bardwell,	130 89	
18.	Joseph Chandler,	110 00	
19.	Elisha Grant,	61 37	
20.	Joseph Shattuck,	119 43	
	Warren Bailey, .	2 00	
21.	Willard Durant,	144 70	
22.	George F. Baker,	139 07	
23.	William D. Stark,	313 75	
	Abbott and Jenkins,	6 92	
24.	Stephen Lovejoy,	45 00	
25.	Charles C. Blunt,	247 75	
	Samuel B. Holt,	3 34	
	Amount carried forward,	$3380 88	$9 60

16

District.		Expended.	Snow.
	Amount brought forward,	$3380 88	$9 60
26.	William S. Jenkins,	248 61	
27.	C. O. Cummings,	124 88	
28.	Robert Stott,	124 99	
		$3879 36	$9 60

REMOVING SNOW FROM SIDEWALKS.

John Cornell,	$20 25	
Henry Burtt,	17 50	
Thomas Smith,	12 00	
		$49 75

BRIDGES.

Frye Village. Abbott and Jenkins,	$134 56	
C. O. Cummings,	2 00	
		$136 56
Ballard Vale. Abbott and Jenkins,		258 74
		$395 30

ELM SQUARE.

T. E. Mayberry, $104 15

LIQUOR DEPARTMENT.

Amount of Stock on hand Feb. 1871,	$195 43	
J. A. Broadhead, liquors,	407 73	
Thomas Smith, salary,	46 86	
Expense of Agency,	1 25	
		$651 27
Less amount of bills owing Feb. 1871,		168 21
		$483 06
Cash received by the Town Treasurer, of the agent,	515 73	
Cash received of the agent for selling state liquors,	23 29	
		539 02
		483 06
Profit for the Town,		$55 96

HAY SCALES.

Fairbanks, Brown, and Co., repairs,	$2 50
George H. Parker, salary,	4 18
Abbott and Jenkins, repairs,	40 38
Ezra Farnham, repairs,	2 50
George H. Bean, salary,	15 00
George H. Bean, tickets,	1 65
	$66 21

NEW ROAD TO DEPOT.

T. E. Mayberry, labor,	$1300 00
Margaret W. Newman, land and fences,	270 00
John Dove, land and fences,	172 00
H. W. French, land and fences,	239 36
George H. Chandler, land and fences,	8 75
Episcopal Society, land and fences,	60 00
	$2050 11

HIGH SCHOOL.

Abbott and Jenkins, labor,	$18051 65
Theodore Voelkers, architect,	11 50
	$18063 15

SPRING GROVE CEMETERY.

John H. Flint, land,	$3000 00
Samuel Raymond, labor,	1000 00
William E. Park, Dedication Sermon,	15 00
Henry Burtt, horses for Committee,	4 50
	$4019 50

ABATEMENT OF TAXES.

Gile and Allen,	$1 67
Albion Yeaw,	4 70
E. K. Jenkins, collector, 1870,	43 45
E. K. Jenkins, collector, 1871,	53 07
Whipple File Manufacturing Company, 1870,	143 81
John Morton, 1871,	1 65
	$248 35

REMITTANCE OF TAXES.

E. K. Jenkins, collector, 1870,	$25 65
E. K. Jenkins, collector, 1871,	144 33
	$169 98

MISCELLANEOUS EXPENSES.

George K. Parker, schooling, North Reading,	$10 62
J. W. Perry, counsel on Punchard School,	50 00
William Marland, postage,	16 30
S. K. Johnson, express,	13 72
Charles Mears, distributing envelopes,	3 00
George S. Cole, posting town warrant,	2 00
Henry Dane, returning deaths,	1 00
George S. Merrill, printing,	147 50
George F. Baker, notifying town officers,	7 00
John Clark, posting town warrants and orders,	24 50
W. F. Draper, printing,	423 04
H. E. Hood, recording deed,	85
Henry C. Harnden, guide-boards,	5 00
S. D. Abbott, bridge plank,	89 50
H. W. French, serving road warrants,	18 00
John Stack, cleaning well,	12 00
Amount carried forward,	$824 03

Amount brought forward,	$824	03
E. K. Jenkins, recording deed,		75
John T. Marland, distributing envelopes,	1	50
Charles C. Holt, pump, Elm Square, .	40	00
Simeon F. Flint, land damage,	14	00
George H. Parker, stationery,	1	90
Robert Callahan, returning deaths,	4	40
E. K. Jenkins, recording births, marriages, and deaths,	42	75
Michael Nolan, returning deaths,	2	30
Asa A. Abbott, surveying,	6	00
Geo. F. Witherell, soldier's grave-stones,	195	00
W. F. Draper, stationery,	21	71
Herman Phelps, returning deaths,		80
Oliver Stevens, counsel before Legislative Committee,	25	00
Abbott and Jenkins watering-trough (Jameson's),	10	50
Abbott and Jenkins, guide-boards,	4	00
J. H. Flint, postage and stationery,	1	77
J. H. Flint, railroad fares,	14	90
E. K. Jenkins, railroad fares, stamps, and stationery,	10	45
E. K. Jenkins, recording,	6	00
George H. Bean, dinners for selectmen and checkers,	8	95
	$1236	71

MEMORIAL HALL.

Abbott and Jenkins, contractors,	15000	00
Samuel Raymond,	317	52
William H. Boardman, stone-work,	1438	50
John Smith, land,	3000	00
Joseph W. Smith, land,	850	00·
Mrs. Sarah Merrill,	800	00
John F. Eaton, architect,	200	00
John Chandler, grading,	440	18
George Foster,	35	89
John Ragan, stone-work,	350	00
David Middleton,	4	00
	$22436	09

SUMMARY OF SELECTMEN'S ORDERS.

Schoolhouses,	$1013 34	
Schools,	10353 11	
		$11366 45
State Aid,	2303 00	
Services of Town Officers,	1942 50	
Liquor Department,	455 84	
Remittance of Taxes,	169 98	
Abatement of Taxes,	248 35	
High Schoolhouse,	18063 15	
Spring Grove Cemetery,	4019 50	
New Road to Depot,	2050 11	
Hay Scales,	66 21	
Town House Expenses,	383 15	
Miscellaneous Expenses,	1236 71	
Fire Department,	3694 14	
Highways,	3879 36	
Removing Snow,	59 35	
Bridges,	395 30	
Elm Square,	104 15	
		39070 80
Memorial Hall,		22436 09
		$72873 34

OVERSEER'S ACCOUNT.

Ann E. Bean,	$72 00
John Fielding,	12 09
Elbridge G. Wardwell,	12 12
Mrs. Sewell Pearsons,	63 13
Abiel Upton,	13 50
Delina Jones,	22 00
Dorcas B. Chandler,	33 00
Mrs. T. C. Mason,	48 00
Family of Patrick Qualey,	3 00
Family of David Goodwin,	18 50
Mrs. E. Mason,	60 47
Mrs. Mary F. Lovejoy,	24 00
Mrs. H. B. Gile,	59 75
Mrs. Trulan,	21 56
Edward Russell,	76 00
Carlton Parker,	21 00
Anna Jones,	39 00
Michael Driscoll,	4 00
Mrs. E. S. Merrill,	1 75
William L. Johnson,	1 75
Osman Jeffcock,	3 00
Samuel W. Abbott,	3 50
Lawrence Bird,	20 58
Barney Barnes, coffin,	5 00
George Mugford, coffin,	8 00
Herman Phelps, burial of George Mugford,	3 00
Herman Phelps, burial of unknown child,	3 00
Herman Phelps, burial of child of Lot Smith,	2 00
Robert Callahan, burial of Susan Goodwin,	5 00
Robert Callahan, burial of Thomas W. Platt,	5 00
	$664 70

PAID CITIES AND TOWNS.

North Reading, Charles B. Abbott,	$53 72
City of Salem, Mrs. Albert Goldsmith,	10 00
City of Boston, Hannah Farrington,	4 50
	$68 22

LUNATIC HOSPITALS.

Northampton, James Duncan,	$197 03
Worcester, Mrs. Solon Johnson,	25 50
Worcester, Luke Worthley,	15 00
	$237 53

DUE FROM CITIES AND TOWNS.

Westford, Mrs. Julius C. Bostwick,	$11 00
Haverhill, Mrs. John Peckcr,	6 00
Newburyport, Rebecca Merrill,	45 75
Lowell, James Death,	19 75
Boston, Elijah Bird,	27 75
	$110 25

EXPENSES OF ALMSHOUSE.

Charles O. Cummings, salary,	$550 00
Charles Mayer, cow and calf,	85 00
Joel Barnes, groceries,	263 52
Holt and Higgins, groceries,	517 19
Farnsworth, Harding, and Co., groceries,	177 32
H. P. Beard and Co., groceries,	302 84
Smith, Manning, and Co., groceries,	262 17
Amount carried forward,	$2158 04

Amount brought forward,	$2158 04
H. W. Abbott, groceries,	28 42
John Findley, fish,	96 43
George Pervere, labor,	132 00
John Cornell, coal,	166 50
Brooks F. Holt, refrigerator,	55 00
Brooks F. Holt, ice.	17 00
John H. Flint, meat,	117 40
Valpey Brothers, meat,	286 57
H. P. Holt, meat,	306 75
William Marland, P. O. box,	1 00
William S. Jenkins, sawing,	60
Thomas Smith, repairing boots and shoes,	23 56
William Poor, repairing wagons,	44 65
John W. Faulkner,	86 23
Annie D. Shannon,	8 15
P. M. Jefferson, soap,	59 94
Gile and Allen, repairs,	3 00
Corse and Stephens,	18 25
E. H. Barnard,	9 70
George H. Parker, medicines,	34 60
W. H. Kimball, medical attendance,	25 00
William Barnett, labor and supplies,	39 80
J. W. Barnard, boots and shoes,	58 11
	$3776 70

SUMMARY OF OVERSEERS' ORDERS.

Expense of Almshouse,	$3776 70
Relief out of Almshouse,	664 70
Paid Cities and Towns,	68 22
Due from Cities and Towns,	110 25
Lunatic Hospitals,	237 53
	$4857 40

REPRESENTATIVE FUND.

In accordance with the wishes of the donor, Edward Taylor, the interest of the above has been applied to the families of Mrs. Goff and Miss Caroline Flint.

JOHN H. FLINT, ⎫ OVERSEERS
BENJ. BOYNTON, ⎬ OF
LEWIS G. HOLT, ⎭ THE POOR.

SUPERINTENDENT'S ACCOUNT.

DR.

To balance from last account,	$31 34
To cash for	
Oxen,	222 53
Labor,	254 20
Hay,	133 57
Vegetables,	153 81
Services of bull,	25 00
Calves,	60 29
Hides and tallow,	19 41
Wood,	6 50
Pigs,	91 00
Keeping cow,	1 50
Lodging prisoners,	5 00
Milk,	10 18
Oat straw,	1 50
Use of plough,	1 00
Board of H. G. Brown,	27 00
Board of James Makinson,	20 00
Board of Margaret Capell,	3 50
	$1067 33

CR.

To cash paid for	
Oxen,	$160 67
Labor,	427 00
Town Treasurer,	257 00
Clothing,	35 87
Grinding corn,	3 96
One pair clamps,	1 50
Calf,	14 00
Amount carried forward,	$900 00

Amount brought forward,	$900 00
To cash paid for	
Washing,	13 05
Medicine,	13 97
Farm tools,	29 33
Barley and grinding,	3 40
Railroad fares and freight,	9 40
One bbl. crackers,	3 60
Cider and vinegar,	5 00
Threshing grain,	6 00
Repairing furniture,	2 80
Repairing wagon and cart,	18 25
Surveying,	50
Balance due the town,	62 03
	$1067 33

CHARLES O. CUMMINGS, SUPERINTENDENT.

ALMSHOUSE.

Whole number of Paupers in Almshouse during the year,	40
Whole number of weeks' board,	1295
Whole number of foreign paupers entertained,	282
Whole number of weeks' board,	81
Whole number of persons held in custody awaiting trial,	11
Whole number of weeks' board of prisoners,	3

REMAINING IN ALMSHOUSE.

Over eighty years old,	1
Between seventy and eighty,	4
Between sixty and seventy,	4
Between fifty and sixty,	2
Between forty and fifty,	3
Between thirty and forty,	1
Between ten and twenty,	5
Between one and ten,	4
	24

Hannah G. Brown died May 30th, 1871, aged forty-seven.
Clarence E. Edwards, born May 13th, 1871.

INVENTORY OF HOUSEHOLD FURNITURE.

Fifty iron bedsteads,	$150 00
Ten stoves,	175 00
Glass and crockery ware, jugs, and jars,	70 00
Chairs, benches, tables, desk, and wooden-ware,	100 00
Beds and bedding, 365.00 ; tin ware, 45.00,	410 00
Table and teaspoons, knives and forks,	30 00
Glass chimneys, and table-linen,	25 00
Kettles, sadirons, clocks, and bells,	14 00
Refrigerator, lamps, and brooms,	60 00
Meat-block, meat-benches, saw, and axe,	15 00
Meat, cider, and apple barrels,	16 50
	$1065 50

PROVISIONS.

Flour, 34.00 ; butter, 35.00 ; oil, 4.60,	$73 60
Lard, 16.00 ; soap, 25.50 ; salt, 2.25,	43 75
Beef, 40.00 ; hams, 25.92 ; salt pork, 82.50,	148 42
Potatoes, 220.00 ; beets, 12.00 ; cranberries, 3.00,	235 00
Vinegar, 4.40 ; pickles, 1.00 ; rice, .40,	5 80
Squashes, 2.50 ; onions, 6.00 ; spices, 2.00,	10 50
Molasses, 2.40 ; raisins, .50 ; preserves, 1.50,	4 40
Coffee, 3.40 ; tea, 36.25 ; sugar, 22.00,	61 65
Crackers, 3.00 ; cream-tarter, 2.75 ; tobacco, 5.76,	11 51
Mustard, soap-powder, and saleratus,	4 50
	$599 13

CLOTHING.

Pants, shawls, dresses, boots, shoes, gloves, and leather,	$75 00

FARM IMPLEMENTS.

Two horse-wagons, harnesses, pung, sleigh, robe, blankets, and whip,	$195 00
Ox-wagon, two ox-carts, sled, and harrows,	180 00
Hay-wagon, stone-trucks, drag, wheelbarrow, chains, and yokes,	88 00
Scythes, sickles, corn-cutters, and hoes,	16 50
Horse, hay, and garden rakes,	18 00
Horse, hay, and manure forks,	25 00
Ox-scraper, ploughs, horse-hoe, cultivator, and mowing-machine,	146 00
Shovels, spades, picks, iron-bars, axes, and blasting-tools,	36 50
Carpenter's tools, wood-saws, beetle-wedges, and ladle,	13 00
Feed-trough, hay-cutter, measures, and feed-boxes,	9 50
Grindstone, ladders, blocks, and ropes,	33 00
Nails, spikes, old iron, and vise,	15 00
Winnowing-mill, meal-bags, and salt-sacks,	15 00
Snow-plough, ox-muzzles, pig-box, and barrels,	16 00
Grain-chests, scalding-tubs, steelyards, baskets, hay-caps, and drain tile,	86 00
	$892 50

FARM PRODUCE.

Oats, corn, rye, beans, hay-seed, meal, and shorts,	$77 55
English and meadow hay, second crop, straw, and corn-fodder,	552 00
Manure,	320 00
	$949 55

FARM STOCK.

Four oxen, five cows, one bull,	$585 00
Horse, eight swine, and twenty fowls,	242 00
	$827 00

FUEL AND LUMBER.

Bridge plank, boards, and other lumber,	$140 00
Dry wood, cut and split, and coal,	290 00
Twenty-three cords hard and soft pinewood,	115 00
	$545 00

SUMMARY.

Inventory of household furniture,	$1065 50
Provisions,	599 13
Clothing,	75 00
Farm implements,	892 50
Farm produce, .	949 55
Farm stock,	827 00
Fuel and lumber,	545 00
	$4953 68

TREASURER'S ACCOUNT.

Town of Andover in account current with E. K. Jenkins, Treasurer,
A. D. 1871.

DR.

To paid County tax for 1871,		$3590 60
State tax for 1871,		7125 00
Interest on town notes,		2305 14
Town notes,		16700 00
Discount on taxes at 6 per cent, $2202 40,		
Discount on taxes at 4 per cent, 126 35,		
		2328 75
Selectmens' orders, current expenses,		39070 80
Selectmens' orders, Schools,		10353 11
Selectmens' orders, Schoolhouses,		1013 34
Overseers of the poor, orders,		4857 40
State Treasurer tax on Andover National Bank Shares (law 1871),		2441 16
Discount on tax on Andover National Bank Shares (law 1871),		109 04
Selectmen and Auditors,		32 00
To balance of taxes unpaid,		804 11
To paid for land and Memorial Hall, per order Committee,		22436 09
To Cash on hand to balance,		12845 29
		$126,011 83

CR.

| By balance of taxes unpaid Feb. 14th, 1871, | $1239 65 |
| By cash on hand Feb. 14th, 1871, | 3962 76 |

By cash received from —

Haverhill pauper account, 1869,	21 00
Newburyport pauper account, 1869,	39 00
Westford pauper account, 1870,	10 00
County Treasurer, discount on County tax,	35 90
Thomas Smith, liquor agent,	539 02
Rent of Town House,	509 00
Rent of stores and hall at Ballardvale,	230 00
John Dove for ventilators,	20 00
John Abbott, treasurer proprietors fund,	96 00
Hiram W. French for old plank,	8 00
C. O. Cummings, Superintendent of Almshouse,	257 00
State Treasurer for State aid,	2200 00
State Treasurer for corporation tax,	8544 24
State Treasurer for National Bank tax (law of 1871),	3677 19
Burial State paupers,	19 50
State Treasurer for school fund,	237 65
County Treasurer for dog licenses,	365 37
Andover National Bank, interest on deposits,	369 41
Hay-scale fees,	56 10
Assessors warrant for Andover National Bank tax (law of 1871),	2550 20
Assessors' warrant for State, County, and Town tax, 1871,	45575 14
Subscriptions for Memorial Hall and Library,	55449 70
	$126,011 83

E. K. JENKINS, TREASURER.

ANDOVER, Feb. 17, 1872.

LIABILITIES.

Notes payable,	$18044 00	
Interest due not called for,	78 00	
Memorial Hall permanent fund,	20000 00	
Memorial Hall building fund,	10013 61	
Memorial Hall library,	3000 00	
		$51135 61

ASSETS.

Cash on hand,	$12845 29	
Taxes unpaid,	804 11	
Cash in Superintendent's hands,	62 03	
Due from cities and towns,	169 50	
Due from Commonwealth for State paupers,	50 58	
Due for State aid,	2486 25	
		$16417 76
Balance against the Town,		$34717 85

SCHEDULE OF TOWN PROPERTY.

Town House and fixtures,	$16000 00
Land under and adjoining,	2000 00
Weights and measures,	200 00
Safe in Town House,	166 00
Hay scales,	300 00
Engine-houses and land,	3636 00
Steam fire-engine and apparatus,	5564 00
Shawshin fire-engine and apparatus at Ballardvale,	1000 00
Town farm and buildings,	6200 00
Personal property, as per inventory,	4953 68
Schoolhouse property,	68139 00
Library,	250 00
	$108408 68

PUNCHARD FREE SCHOOL.

The undersigned, Trustees of the Punchard Free School, herewith render to the Town their Annual Account of the condition of the Fund, and of the Receipts and Expenditures thereof for the year ending February 1st, 1872.

Amount of Permanent Fund as per last Report,	$40,000 00
Amount added thereto from Building Fund,	14,800 00
Present Amount,	$54,800 00

All of which is invested in Valid Notes and Real Estate Securities.

RECEIPTS.

Balance of cash on hand, as per last Report,	$1051 00	
Interest received since said Report from investments,	3428 48	
Interest received of Trustees under the Will of B. H. Punchard, on Twenty Thousand Dollars from March 30, 1871, to January 1, 1872,	903 33	
Cash from Building Fund account,	4162 19	
		$9545 00

EXPENDITURES.

Cash paid :

William G. Goldsmith, Principal,	$916 67
Fanny L. D. Strong, Assistant,	233 33
Ellen T. Brown, Assistant,	166 67
Moses Foster, Treasurer,	100 00
Cyrus Brown, agent, for Insurance,	645 00
Hallett, Davis, and Co., Piano Forte,	367 00
Tucker Manufacturing Co., Chandeliers, etc.,	119 03
A. Clark and Son, Telescope,	300 00
James L. Ross, School Furniture, etc.,	1501 92
H.B. & W.O.Chamberlain, Philosophical Apparatus,	206 75
G. B. Cartwright, Venetian Blinds,	524 80
E. T. Ritchie and Son, Philosophical Apparatus,	466 14
J. F. Babcock and Co., Chemical Apparatus,	49 36
Amount carried forward,	$5596 67

5

34

Amount brought forward,	$5596	67
C. Stodder, Microscope,	98	75
C. Wakefield, Mats and Matting,	86	86
S. Williams and Co., Globe,	44	00
D. Pratt and Son, Clocks,	56	50
George Terrill, Curtains,	99	70
W. P. Prescott, account,	7	00
Thomas Groom, and Co., Stationery,	6	00
American Tablet Co., account,	6	75
Cole and Young, Rubber Moulding,	80	00
Boston and Maine Railroad, Freight,	30	40
John Cornell, coal,	190	00
Thomas Smith, Janitor, etc.,	75	00
William Barnett, account,	30	24
N. W. Hazen, Globes, etc., lost at fire,	42	00
John Sullivan, labor,	23	50
B. S. White, account,	9	88
Abbott and Jenkins, balance of account,	118	60
J. H. Cochran, account,	3	00
Samuel Woodman, account,	2	40
Henry Jaquith, account,	2	00
Thomas Hall, Chemicals,	14	50
George S. Merrill and Co., account,	4	00

$6627 75

Cash deposited in Andover National Bank to balance, 2917 25

$9545 00

Respectfully submitted,

CHARLES SMITH,   NATHAN FRYE,
JAMES H. MERRILL,   JOHN ABBOTT,
JAMES THOMPSON,   EDWARD TAYLOR,
MOSES FOSTER,   BENJ'N BOYNTON.

ANDOVER, February 1st, 1872.

REPORT

OF THE

CEMETERY COMMITTEE.

THE undersigned Cemetery Committee, chosen July 6th, 1869, respectfully report that at a Town Meeting, held May 2d, 1871, the following resolution and votes were passed.

Resolved, That the votes of the Town heretofore passed, setting apart a portion of the Town land and certain additions to be purchased of Messrs Flint and Foster for a Cemetery be, and are hereby, rescinded.

Voted, That the Cemetery Committee be authorized to purchase of John H. Flint et als., their lot of forty-one acres, more or less, situated on the east side of the old road leading to Ballard Vale, for a sum not exceeding three thousand dollars, and that the same be dedicated to the purposes of a Cemetery, and be improved by the Committee for that purpose.

Voted, That all sums of money heretofore voted by the Town for the improvement of the " Carmel Hill " lot, be transferred and expended in the improvement of the new lot this day designated for a Cemetery; and that the Selectmen be authorized and directed to draw their warrant on the Town Treasurer for a sum not exceeding four thousand dollars, to pay for the above-named land, and the improvements to be made upon it, when requested so to do by the Committee.

In accordance with the authority and instruction given us by the foregoing votes, the Committee purchased of John H. Flint and others, the lot of land referred to, consisting of forty-one acres, for three thousand dollars. They then commenced improvements, by laying out the grounds, making avenues sixteen feet wide and paths nine feet wide, the length of both being about half a mile. The soil, to the depth of eight inches, was taken out, and gravel put in ; the old railroad track has been cleared of brush, and the lower parts of it filled up. Nearly three hundred feet of wall on the eastern side of said track have been re-set, draining laid, and the underbrush cleared from three fourths of the premises west of the track. A portion of the land has been laid out into nearly one hundred lots, of various sizes, so arranged as to leave ample space in front, rear, and sides of the lots.

At a Town Meeting held August 7th, 1871, By-Laws, Rules, and Regulations for the proper care, improvement, and protection of said Cemetery were passed. The first section reads as follows: " The location selected and purchased by the Cemetery, Committee under the authority of the vote of the Town of Andover shall be designated and known as ' Spring Grove Cemetery.' " A part of the seventh section is as follows : " It shall be the duty of said Committee to submit annually a written Report of their doings, comprising a statement of all monies received and expended on account of said Cemetery, which Report shall be printed in connection with the Auditors' annual Report."

The Grove was formally dedicated, October 15th 1871, and a very able and interesting address was delivered on the occasion by Rev. William E. Park, of Lawrence, a native of this town. A few days subsequently the choice of lots was offered at auction, and several were taken. The number selected by parties is eleven, and the deeds of conveyance of five have been passed.

Amount received from the Town Treasurer,		$4000 00
Amount received for lots,		100 00
		$4100 00
Paid to John H. Flint, and others, for		
land, - - - - - -	- 3000 00	
Paid for improvements and expenses,	1099 63	
		$4099 63
In hands of Committee,		37

There are now outstanding bills against the Committee amounting to about one hundred and thirty dollars. It will be necessary the ensuing year to lay out and improve other portions of the land; cut a head avenue, procure and erect stone posts and gates; trim up the grove; set out ornamental trees, build wing walls, and repair fences. The Committee, therefore, recommend that the Town make an appropriation, not exceeding two thousand dollars, for the purposes indicated.

WM. G. MEANS,
EDWARD TAYLOR,
NATHAN FRYE,
MOSES FOSTER,
GEORGE FOSTER,
WILLIAM S. JENKINS,
E. FRANCIS HOLT.

ANDOVER, Feb. 14, 1872.

The foregoing Accounts having been carefully examined, and found to have been correctly kept and well vouched, we respectfully present our Report to the Town for acceptance. In taking the inventory of the personal property at the Almshouse the Auditors noticed the need of painting and papering the rooms, and that there is a deficiency of furniture in the house. An expenditure for these purposes seem to be desirable.

GEORGE H. VALPEY, ⎫
GEORGE FOSTER, ⎬ AUDITORS.
HENRY BOYNTON, ⎭

ANDOVER, Feb. 17, 1872.

TOWN WARRANT.

ESSEX, SS. To JOHN CLARK, one of the Constables of the Town of Andover, GREETING :

In the name of the Commonwealth of Massachusetts, you are hereby directed to notify and warn the inhabitants of the Town of Andover, qualified to vote in elections and town affairs, to meet and assemble at the Town House in said Andover, on Monday, the Fourth day of March, 1872, at One o'clock, P. M., to act on the following Articles, namely :

Article 1st. — To choose a Moderator to preside at said meeting.

Article 2d. — To choose a Town Clerk for the year ensuing.

Article 3d. — To hear and act on the Report of the Auditors.

Article 4th. — To choose Selectmen, Assessors, Overseers of the Poor, Town Treasurer, School Committee, Constables, Fence Viewers, and all other necessary and usual Town Officers.

Article 5th. — To see what sum of money the Town will raise for the repairs of Highways the ensuing year.

Article 6th. — To see if the Town will choose Road Commissioners to take charge of the repairs of the Highways, Roads, and Bridges of the Town, or what method they will adopt for said repairs.

Article 7th. — To see if the Town will require the appointment of a Superintendent of Schools, as provided in Chap. 38, Sec. 35 of the General Statutes of Massachusetts.

Article 8th. — To see what sum of money the Town will raise for the maintenance of their Public Schools for the ensuing year.

Article 9th. — To see what method the Town will adopt to apportion the School money among the Public Schools.

Article 10th. — To see what sum of money the Town will raise for the repairs and improvement of the School Property, and for Incidental Expenses of the Schoolhouses.

Article 11th. — To see what sum of money the Town will raise to defray the necessary Expenses the year ensuing.

Article 12th. — To see what sum of money the Town will raise towards paying the Town Debt.

Article 13th. — To see what method the Town will adopt for the collection of the Public Taxes the ensuing year.

Article 14th. — To see if the Town will authorize the Town Treasurer to hire money for the use of the Town when necessary.

Article 15th. — To see what compensation the Town will pay the Firemen for their services the ensuing year.

Article 16th. — To see if the Town will appropriate the sum of One Hundred and Fifty Dollars to defray the expense of decorating Soldiers' Graves.

Article 17th. — To see if the Town will authorize the Selectmen to purchase the Land under and adjoining the South Centre Schoolhouse.

Article 18th. — To hear a Report and recommendation from the Memorial Hall Building Committee, and to see what action the Town will take in relation thereto.

Article 19th. — To hear a Report of the Selectmen on building a Reservoir in Elm Square.

Article 20th. — To see if the Town will make an appropriation in behalf of the Cemetery, as recommended in the Report of the Committee.

Article 21st. — To see if the Town, will instruct the Selectmen to make a suitable entrance from Central Street to the New Road leading from Centre Schoolhouse to the Boston and Main Railroad, and to remove the gravel and other materials at the Northerly end of the new Street which has not been already provided for, and to finish the Street according to the directions of the County Commissioners.

Article 22d. — To see if the Town will discontinue a piece of old Road near the house of Asa W. Livingston.

Article 23d. — To see if the Town will accept and revise the List of Jurors, as prepared and posted by the Selectmen.

Article 24th. — To act on any other business that may legally come before said meeting.

Hereof fail not, and make due return of this Warrant, with your doings thereon, to the Town Clerk, at the time and place of meeting.

Given under our hands, at Andover, this Twenty-third day of February, in the year of our Lord one thousand eight hundred and seventy-two.

JOHN H. FLINT,   ⎫ Selectmen
BENJ. BOYNTON,   ⎬   of
LEWIS G. HOLT,   ⎭ Andover.

A true Copy. — Attest:

JOHN CLARK,
Constable of Andover.

CPSIA information can be obtained
at www.ICGtesting.com
Printed in the USA
BVHW091236261118
534010BV00012B/323/P